HOW OUR BODIES WORK

THE HEART AND BLOOD

JAN BURGESS

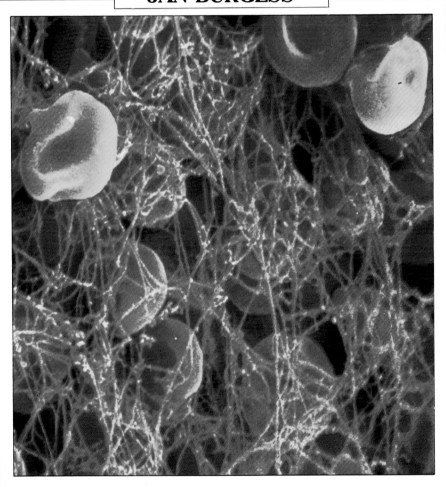

Editorial planning
Philip Steele

SILVER BURDETT PRESS

Copyright © 1988 by Schoolhouse Press, Inc.
an imprint of Silver Burdett Press Inc.
Prentice Hall Building, Route 9W,
Englewood Cliffs, N.J. 07632

Original copyright, © Macmillan Education Limited 1988
© BLA Publishing Limited 1988

Designed and produced by BLA Publishing Limited,
Swan Court, East Grinstead, Sussex, England.

A Ling Kee Company

Illustrations by Anna Hancock; Sallie Alane Reason and Linda
Thursby/Linden Artists
Color origination by Waterden Reproductions
Printed in Hong Kong

93   6 5 4 3 2

Library of Congress Cataloging-in-Publication

Burgess, Janet, 1952–
    The heart and blood.
    (How our bodies work)
    Includes index.
    Summary: Discusses how the heart and circulatory system
work, the functions of blood, how doctors help people with
blood and heart disorders, and how to keep the cardiovascular
system healthy through diet and exercise.
    1. Cardiovascular system — Juvenile literature.
2. Blood — Juvenile literature. 3. Heart — Juvenile
literature. [1. Cardiovascular system. 2. Blood.
3. Heart] I. Title. II. Series

QP103.B87   1988   612'.1   87-35744
ISBN 0-382-09700-9 (hardback)

Photographic credits

t = top b = bottom l = left r = right

cover: Trevor Hill

4 Science Photo Library; 6 The Hutchison Library;
7 Vivien Fifield; 8*t* Royal College of Physicians;
8*b* Science Photo Library; 9 Ann Ronan Picture Library;
10 Science Photo Library; 13 J. Allan Cash; 14 Biophoto
Associates; 15 Vision International; 16 S. & R. Greenhill;
17*t* Science Photo Library; 17*b* S. & R. Greenhill;
19 J. Allan Cash; 20 Biophoto Associates; 21*t*, 21*b*, 22
Science Photo Library; 23 S. & R. Greenhill; 26 Frank
Lane Picture Agency; 27*t* Vision International; 27*b* S. &
R. Greenhill; 29*t* Vision International; 29*b* LAT
Photographic; 31 Science Photo Library; 32*l*, 32*r*
Biophoto Associates; 33*t* J. Allan Cash; 33*b*, 34, 35*t*, 35*b*
Science Photo Library; 36 St Bartholomew's Hospital;
37 Dr T. Korn/Ysbyty Gwynedd; 38, 39*t*, 39*b* Science
Photo Library; 42 S. & R. Greenhill; 44*t* ZEFA; 44*b*
Vision International; 45 S. & R. Greenhill

How To Use This Book:
This book has many useful features. For example, look at the table of contents. See how it describes each section in the book. Find a section you want to read and turn to it.

Notice that the section is a "two-page spread." That is, it covers two facing pages. Now look at the headings in the spread. Headings are useful when you want to locate specific information. Next, look at a photograph, drawing, chart or map and find its caption. Captions give you additional information. A chart or map may also have labels to help you.

Scan the spread for a word in **bold print**. If you cannot find one in this spread, find one in another spread. Bold-print words are defined in the glossary at the end of the book. Find your bold-print word in the glossary.

Now turn to the index at the end of the book. When you have a specific topic or subject to research, look for it in the index. you will quickly know whether the topic is in the book.

We hope you will use the features in this book to help you learn about new and exciting things.

Contents

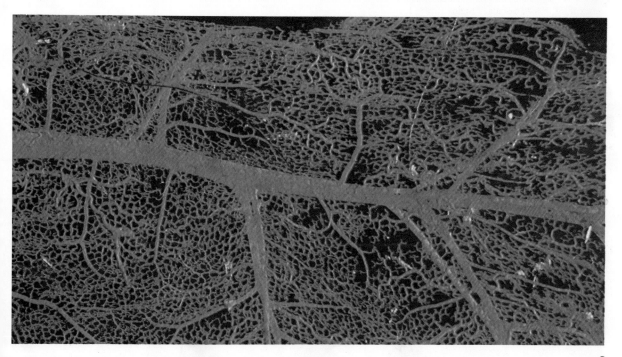

Introduction

In the middle of your chest is your **heart**. It started beating when you were still inside your mother. This was about seven months before you were born. Your heart has kept beating since then whether you have been asleep or awake. It will go on beating until you die. The heart does not always beat at the same speed. In an adult, the heart beats 60 to 80 times a minute. A child's heart beats 80 to 100 times a minute.

Keeping Us Alive

Bones called the **ribs** make a strong shield around your heart. The central bone, or **sternum**, helps to protect it, too. An adult's heart is about the size of a clenched fist. A child's heart is smaller. It grows as the child grows.

The heart pumps a red liquid called **blood** to every part of the body. It pushes the blood from the roots of your hair to the tips of your toes and back again. Every part of your body needs blood. If any part of the body is cut off from its blood supply, it dies. It is very important for the heart to keep pumping blood.

When parts of your body are very active, they need extra blood. Then, the heart must work faster to pump the extra blood to that area. The heartbeat gets faster. Instead of beating 70 times a minute, an adult's heart may beat up to 100 times a minute.

A child's heart can beat even faster. For example, when you ride your bicycle uphill, you get short of breath and your legs feel tired. Your leg muscles need more blood than usual. Your heart must pump faster to supply that extra blood. You can feel your heart thumping in your chest. Once you have reached the top of the hill, you quickly get your breath back. Your heartbeat slows down to normal again.

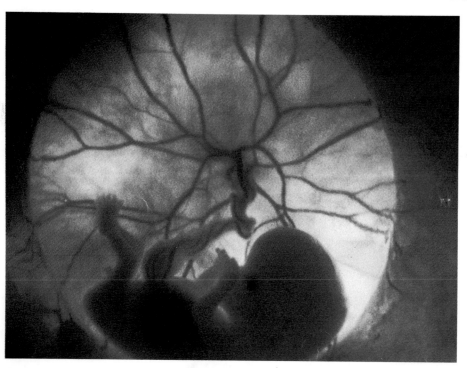

◄ Blood keeps us alive even before we are born. It helps babies grow when they are still inside their mother. The heart sends blood to every part of the baby's body.

Lessons to Learn

This book explains how the heart works and why blood is so important. Also, it explains how you can take care of your heart. Our hearts usually continue to work without a problem all our lives.

Sometimes, however, things go wrong. Heart disease is a growing problem in some countries. Doctors are finding out new things all the time about heart problems. They already know that people should take care of their hearts when they are young. If they do they may prevent heart disease later on.

Different kinds of animals have various ways of pumping blood around their bodies. Each system has developed to suit the needs of the animal. The human heart has developed to suit the kind of life we lead. Birds need a lot of energy in order to fly, which means that their bodies need a rapid supply of blood. Birds have hearts which are very large for their body size, and which beat very fast.

▼ You can feel your heart beating on the left hand side of your chest when you are out of breath. It works together with the other parts of your body. The heart keeps us alive by pumping blood through the body.

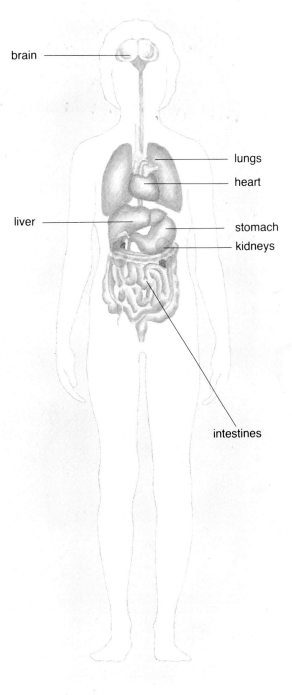

The First Healers

▼ A Buddhist monk treats a snake bite. Modern scientists have told us how the body works, and have found many wonderful cures for illness. However, in many parts of the world, healing methods are used that are thousands of years old.

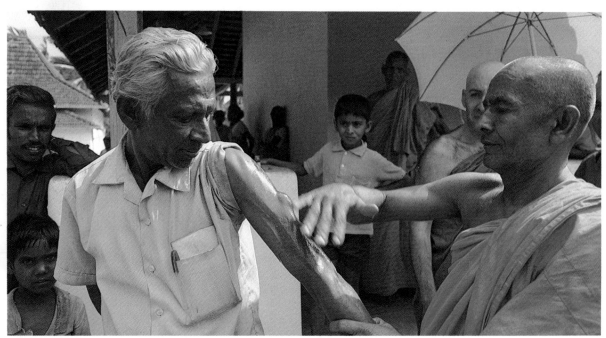

Long ago, there were no doctors or nurses to take care of people when they became sick. There were no books with good advice. People could only do simple things to make the sick feel better. They might wash a cut or make a soothing drink from plants. It was hard to understand why some people got better with this treatment, while others did not. Many people believed that it was bad magic that made them sick, and good magic that made them better.

Early Doctors

The first doctors used all kinds of things to make medicines. The medicines were made from plants, minerals, insects, and animals like mice and frogs. Some doctors believed that if a plant had heart-shaped leaves, it must be good for the heart.

About 2,500 years ago, doctors began to figure out new ways to treat patients. In ancient Egypt, there were different doctors for different parts of the body. The most famous doctor in ancient Greece was Hippocrates. He is often called the father of modern medicine. He believed, incorrectly, that the veins carried air around the body. He also believed that there were fluids called **humors** in the body. If people had the wrong amounts of these humors in their bodies they would get sick. One of these humors was blood.

Another famous Greek doctor named Galen cut open, or **dissected**, the bodies of dead animals to study them. He wrote many books. Doctors followed his ideas for hundreds of years. We now know that some of the things Galen taught were wrong. For example, he thought that the heart heated up the blood. He also thought that blood flowed backwards and forwards through the body like ocean tides.

▶ Early doctors knew that the heart and blood were important, but they understood little about how the body worked. Their patients often died.

Searching for the Truth

Doctors in other parts of the world were also finding out about how the body works. Early Chinese doctors knew that blood travels around the body. They also checked the health of their patients by listening to their heartbeats. It was a long time before such ideas were tried out in the West.

Vesalius was a doctor and teacher who lived in Italy 400 years ago. He dissected human bodies and found out that the blood is carried through the body by tubes. He proved that many of the old ideas about medicine were wrong.

Hearts and Flowers

Many of the ideas that doctors had about how the body works seem strange to us now. One idea was that different parts of the body could make us have different feelings. The heart was supposed to control our feelings of love. Even now, people still connect the heart with the idea of love. People talk about having a broken heart when they are very unhappy, and some people send Valentine's Day cards with hearts on them to people they love. However, people today know that the heart is really just another part of the body.

Finding Out

People understood that the heart and blood were important. If someone was sick, he or she might be given the blood of certain animals to drink. People were often bled. Doctors thought the sickness would leak out with the blood, and that **bloodletting** would balance the humors in the body.

In 1628, a man named William Harvey was the first to find out that the heart is a pump which pushes blood through tubes called **blood vessels**. He noticed that some vessels take blood away from the heart, while others bring it back. He also noticed that there are tiny doors called **valves** in some of the blood vessels. They only open in one direction. Harvey discovered that blood flows around the body all the time. This is called **circulation**.

▲ William Harvey was a doctor at St. Bartholomew's Hospital in London. He was the first person to explain how blood traveled around the body. Harvey is shown here explaining his ideas to the King.

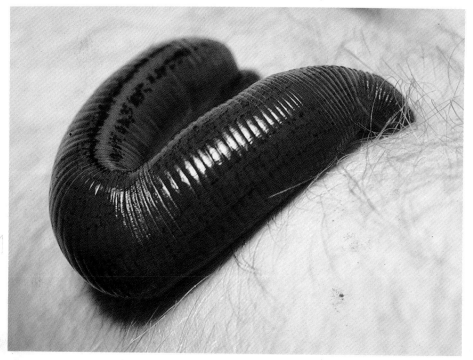

◄ Doctors kept water creatures called leeches specially for bloodletting. The leeches were put on the patient's skin. They sucked out some of the patient's blood. When the leeches were full, they dropped off. They could be used again later.

More Discoveries

Harvey's work made it easier to understand how the heart and blood work. Some doctors took blood from one animal and gave it to another. This is called a blood **transfusion**. Then, they tried blood transfusions between animals and people. Often, these experiments killed the patients, because there are different kinds of blood and it is dangerous to mix them in the body. Soon, it was against the law in Europe to transfuse blood. It was not until a hundred years ago that doctors figured out how to do blood transfusions safely.

Anton van Leeuwenhoek was a Dutchman born in 1632. He was one of the first people to use a **microscope**. A microscope makes things look larger. Leeuwenhoek saw that blood is made of tiny bits. These tiny bits are blood **cells**. Being able to look at blood so closely helped scientists learn more about what it does.

▼ The first microscopes did not look like the ones doctors use today. Anton van Leeuwenhoek made some which could make tiny objects look 300 times larger. Doctors could now examine blood and see what it was made of.

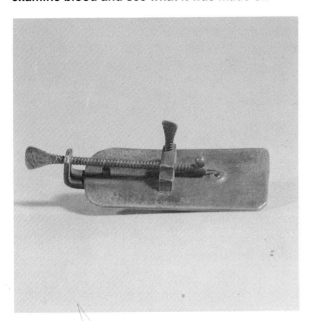

Hearing the Heart

We cannot see inside our bodies, but we can hear what is going on. René Laënnec was a French doctor who lived nearly 200 years ago. He was taking care of a patient who he thought might have heart disease. He had to listen to her heartbeat, so he rolled up a newspaper. He put one end to his ear and the other to her chest. He found that he could hear her heartbeat very clearly. Laënnec went on to make a wooden tube or **stethoscope**. Today, doctors use stethoscopes based on Laënnec's idea to listen to their patients' hearts.

▲ This is how Leeuwenhoek used his microscope. The lens was raised to the eye. The position of the object could be adjusted with the screw.

Around the Body

Your body is made of millions of cells. Cells of the same kind grow together, and build into **tissue**. Different kinds of tissue make up our skin, muscles, nerves, and other **organs**. Whatever kind of tissue it is, it needs fuel to stay alive. The food you eat is the fuel that keeps your body going. Your body breaks the food up into very tiny pieces. These tiny food pieces are separated into useful substances, called **nutrients**, and into waste.

Blood takes the nutrients and many other important things to every part of the body. Blood also carries away any waste matter from your body.

▼ Try taking someone's pulse. Do not use your thumb, because it has a pulse of its own. Use a watch to find out the pulse rate.

A Breath of Fresh Air

When you breathe in you take in air. In air is a gas called **oxygen**. The oxygen goes down into your **lungs** which are the organs in your body used for breathing. Inside the lungs there are millions of tiny blood vessels. The blood flowing through the blood vessels picks up the oxygen. Then, the blood flows to the heart.

Next, the heart pumps the oxygen-rich blood out to the body through a large blood vessel. This branches out into smaller and smaller tubes. They lead to every part of the body. The blood passes its oxygen from the smallest blood vessels to the tissues.

Used blood, with no oxygen left in it, comes back to the heart. The heart pumps the used blood back to the lungs. There, the blood picks up more oxygen and is pumped around the body all over again.

The Blood Carriers

The tubes that carry blood from your heart to the rest of your body are called **arteries**. The blood in the arteries is full of oxygen. This makes the blood look bright red. The arteries divide up into smaller and smaller branches. The smallest of all are called **capillaries**. This is where the blood gives up its oxygen, and takes in waste matter. The color of the blood changes to dark red. The tubes bringing blood back to the heart are called **veins**.

The Body Beat

You can both hear and feel the beat of your heart as it pumps the blood through your arteries. This beat is called the **pulse**. Put the tips of the first two fingers of one hand on the inside of your other wrist. Find the place just below the bone coming down from your thumb. You can feel your pulse beating there. Count the number of beats you feel in a minute. This number is your **pulse rate**.

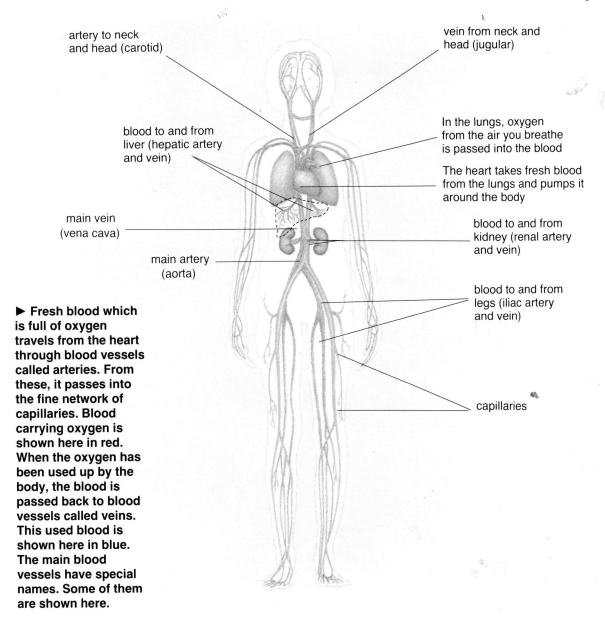

artery to neck
and head (carotid)

vein from neck and
head (jugular)

blood to and from
liver (hepatic artery
and vein)

In the lungs, oxygen
from the air you breathe
is passed into the blood

The heart takes fresh blood
from the lungs and pumps it
around the body

main vein
(vena cava)

blood to and from
kidney (renal artery
and vein)

main artery
(aorta)

blood to and from
legs (iliac artery
and vein)

capillaries

▶ **Fresh blood which
is full of oxygen
travels from the heart
through blood vessels
called arteries. From
these, it passes into
the fine network of
capillaries. Blood
carrying oxygen is
shown here in red.
When the oxygen has
been used up by the
body, the blood is
passed back to blood
vessels called veins.
This used blood is
shown here in blue.
The main blood
vessels have special
names. Some of them
are shown here.**

Did you know

☆ that a normal heart beats about 2.5 billion times in an average lifetime?

☆ that there are more than 60,000 miles of blood vessels in a human body?

☆ that a drop of blood goes around the body more than 1,000 times a day?

☆ that it takes just one minute for a drop of blood to go from your heart, down to your toes, and all the way back again?

☆ that blood leaves the heart traveling at three feet per second?

☆ that a baby has only about one quart of blood; a child has about three quarts of blood; an adult has about five quarts of blood?

How the Heart Works

The heart is a big, powerful **muscle**. It squeezes blood out to the body, like you squeeze dishwashing liquid from a plastic bottle. The heart muscle has to be strong because it pushes blood along thousands of miles of blood vessels all the time.

If you could see the inside of your heart, you would see four different spaces called **chambers**. There are two at the top and two at the bottom. The two at the top are the smaller chambers. They are the left **atrium** and the right atrium. The two at the bottom are the larger chambers. They are called left and right **ventricles**. A wall of muscle down the middle divides the heart into two. It is called the **septum**.

Dark, red used blood collects in the right atrium. When that chamber is full, the blood passes down into the right ventricle. From there, the blood is squeezed out to the lungs. In the lungs, it fills up with oxygen. Then, the fresh, bright red blood goes back to the heart. It collects in the left atrium. Then, the blood is passed down into the left ventricle. The muscle here is the thickest and strongest of all.

All this happens in one complete heartbeat. The left atrium and right atrium squeeze at the same time, passing blood down to the bottom of the heart. A fraction of a second later, the ventricles also squeeze. They send blood shooting out to the lungs and all over the body. The blood in the left side of the heart is full of oxygen. The blood in the right side is without oxygen. Blood from the two sides does not mix.

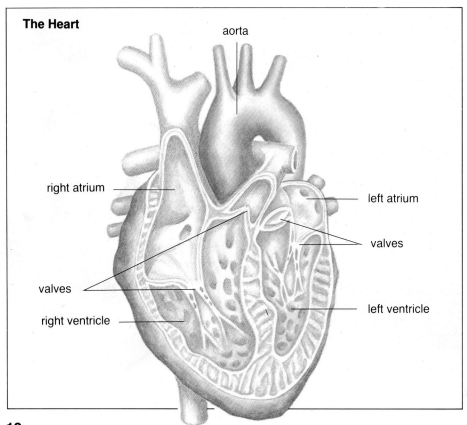

The Heart

aorta

right atrium

left atrium

valves

valves

left ventricle

right ventricle

◀ **Blood collects in each atrium. From there, it passes down to the ventricle on the same side. The right ventricle sends blood to the lungs. The left ventricle pumps blood from the lungs around the body.**

The Steady Beat

Blood could not travel smoothly through the heart without valves. These are tiny flaps of tissue which only open one way. They stop the blood from flowing back the wrong way. When doctors listen to the heartbeat with a stethoscope, they hear a double beat as the heart valves shut tightly.

Inside the heart, there is a part which sends out electrical signals. It is a tiny **pacemaker**. The signals tell the heart when to beat. Sometimes, the body's own pacemaker does not work properly. This may happen when a person gets older or becomes sick. The pacemaker can no longer keep the heart beating at the right rate.

▼ Here, you can see how blood flows in and out of the heart. The movements of blood can take place because there are valves which shut off one part of the heart from another.

▲ Athletes feel tired and out of breath after a race. Their hearts must beat faster to supply the body with the extra oxygen it needs when it has been working hard.

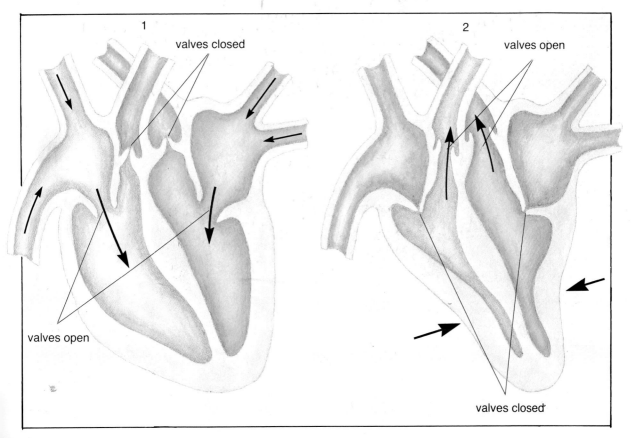

1

valves closed

valves open

2

valves open

valves closed

Blood Vessels

There are millions and millions of cells in your body. Every single cell needs oxygen and nutrients.

Blood carries the oxygen and nutrients to each cell. Blood vessels are the body's transportation system. The blood vessels make it possible for blood to go to every part of the body.

Arteries

Arteries carry blood away from the heart. When the heart squeezes, it pumps blood out to the arteries with great force. The blood is under **pressure**. Arteries have to stand up to this pressure. They have strong, elastic walls. They expand as the blood surges through them. They spring back into shape between heartbeats.

▼ These capillaries are carrying blood to the kidneys. A fine network of these tiny tubes carries oxygen-rich blood to cells all over the body.

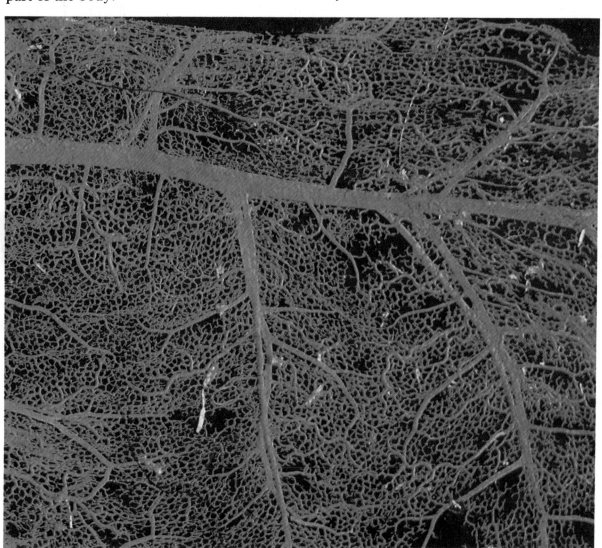

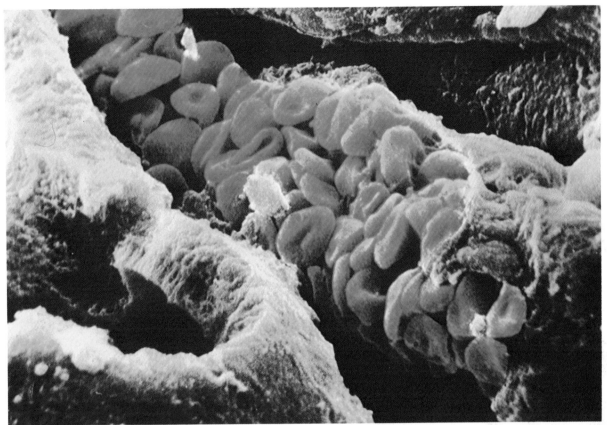

Branching Out

The arteries divide up into smaller branches called **arterioles**. The arterioles divide up into even smaller tubes we call capillaries. The capillaries are so tiny that we can only see them through a microscope. The walls of capillaries are very thin. They are so thin that oxygen and nutrients can seep through into the cells around them. Waste matter can seep back into the capillaries.

Keeping up the Flow

The capillaries join up again with thicker tubes. These are the veins which bring blood back to the heart. The blood in the veins is no longer under pressure. The walls of veins are not as strong or as elastic as those of arteries.

There is no push from the heart to keep the blood flowing up the veins. The muscles

▲ This photograph was taken with a powerful microscope. It allows us to see the tiny blood cells as they carry oxygen through the capillaries.

around the veins do the work. The muscles in your legs and the muscles you use to breathe all help to keep the blood flowing. Inside the veins, the tiny valves prevent the blood from flowing backwards. This is very useful when blood must travel "uphill."

Control systems in the body check that the right amount of blood is going to the places that need it. For example, if not enough blood is reaching one of your feet, that foot soon feels cold and prickly. This uncomfortable feeling will make you change position, so the blood can better reach your foot.

Pressure and Pulse

▼ Take your pulse before and after exercise. The pulse rate will be faster afterwards. The faster rate shows that your heart is working hard to rush blood to your muscles.

The push given to the blood by the heart is called **blood pressure**. Each time the heart beats, this wave of pressure flows outward along the arteries. That wave of pressure is still there as the blood goes up into your head, or down to your feet.

If your heart beats faster, then the pulse is faster, too. Find out your normal pulse rate. Now run or skip hard. Check your pulse again. The pulse rate rises because the muscles you have used for running or skipping need extra food and oxygen. They get this extra food and oxygen from extra blood. The heart has to pump faster to supply these muscles with the extra blood.

The Living Force

Blood pressure is stronger in arteries than in veins, because the heart is pushing the blood out to the far ends of the body. The artery walls are made up of an elastic material. When it is pushed outward by blood pressure it squeezes back into shape. This helps push the blood along. Blood pressure forces the blood into the tiny capillaries. By the time the blood reaches the veins, much of the pressure has been used up. This means that the blood pressure in veins is lower than it is in arteries. Veins are not as elastic as arteries so do not help to maintain the blood pressure.

Then, the doctor takes another measurement. The air in the band is let out a little more. This time, the doctor finds the point that the band begins to let the blood through between the heartbeats, as well as during the heartbeats.

A measurement of blood pressure is always given as two numbers, for example $90/60$. The higher number is the pressure when the heart squeezes. The lower number is the pressure between heartbeats.

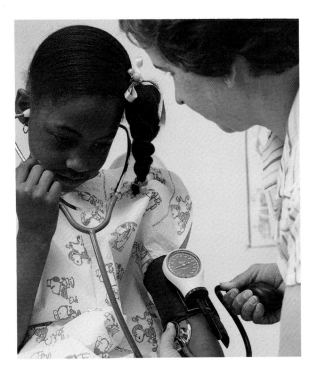

▲ This girl is having her blood pressure taken. The arm band and pressure gauge can be seen on her arm. The doctor has let the girl listen through the stethoscope to her pulse.

Taking Blood Pressure

Doctors check blood pressure because it is one way for them to tell whether a person is healthy or not. They use an inflatable band that goes around your upper arm. A tube from the band leads to a machine that measures pressure. This is called a pressure gauge. The doctor puts the band around the patient's arm, and pumps the band up. The band flattens the artery in the patient's arm, and stops blood from flowing through it.

Then, the doctor lets the air out of the band just enough for the blood to push its way through when the heart beats. The doctor can tell when the blood is coming through by listening with a stethoscope. The pressure of the blood at this point shows on the pressure gauge.

▼ Blood keeps going around your body no matter which way up you are. However, if you stand on your head for long, you will begin to feel uncomfortable. You will get red in the face from the build up of blood in your head. When you stand up, you will soon start to feel normal again.

Blood and the Lungs

Air comes into the body through the lungs. The lungs are like balloons that suck air in and out. It is very important that they keep working. Without the oxygen from the air that they take in, our body cells would die.

The lungs take up most of the space in your chest. They are protected by the cage of the ribs, and the heart lies between the lungs. A network of blood vessels runs from the heart to the lungs and back again.

Taking in Oxygen

When we breathe in, muscles between the ribs lift the rib cage upward and outward. There is another muscle under the lungs. It is a large sheet of muscle called the **diaphragm**. When we breathe in, this flattens and pulls downwards. The space in the lungs gets larger. Air rushes in. When we breathe out, the diaphragm relaxes. This lets the lungs get smaller, and air is pushed out.

The inside of the lungs is similar to a sponge. There are masses of tiny sacks called **alveoli** linked by little tunnels. There are about 750 million aveoli in the lungs. The lungs are filled with air and covered with capillaries. Oxygen from the air seeps into the capillaries from the alveoli. Then, blood full of oxygen goes back to the heart.

In the tiny blood vessels inside the lungs, another important change takes place. While taking in oxygen, the capillaries also get rid of a gas called **carbon dioxide**. Carbon dioxide is waste which is made in every single cell. It has to be removed from the body. We get rid of carbon dioxide when we breathe out. Our blood carries carbon dioxide back to the lungs from all over the body.

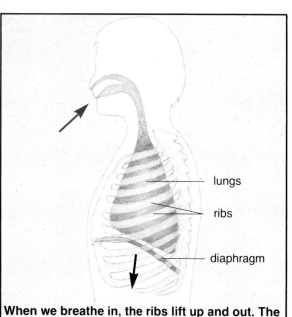

When we breathe in, the ribs lift up and out. The diaphragm pulls down and the space inside the lungs gets bigger. Air is sucked down into the space.

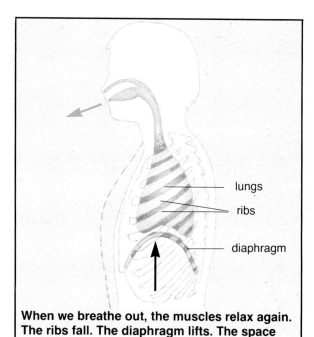

When we breathe out, the muscles relax again. The ribs fall. The diaphragm lifts. The space inside the lungs gets smaller and air is pushed out.

The Lifeline

We take oxygen into the body and we get rid of carbon dioxide. The oxygen is needed by our body cells. The cells use it in a process called **respiration**. Respiration turns oxygen and nutrients into energy in the cells. We need energy for growing, playing, working, and staying alive. Blood is the lifeline between the air and every tiny cell in the body.

▶ We need plants, and not just for food. They have tiny oxygen factories in their leaves. They take in our waste carbon dioxide from the air, and give off the oxygen that we need to breathe.

▼ We have two lungs. Each contains millions of alveoli. From these, oxygen passes into the capillaries which are shown here in red. The capillaries shown here in blue pass carbon dioxide from stale blood back into the alveoli.

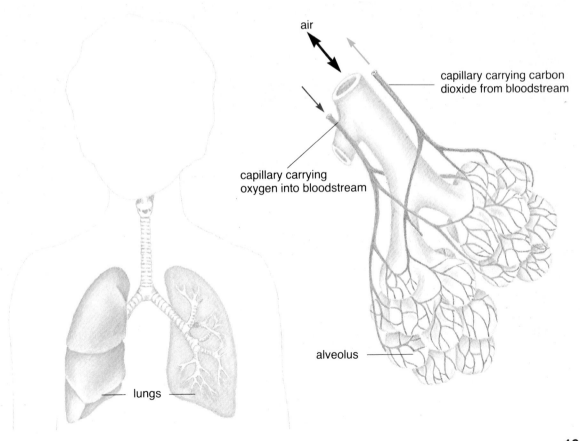

air

capillary carrying carbon dioxide from bloodstream

capillary carrying oxygen into bloodstream

alveolus

lungs

What Is Blood Made Of?

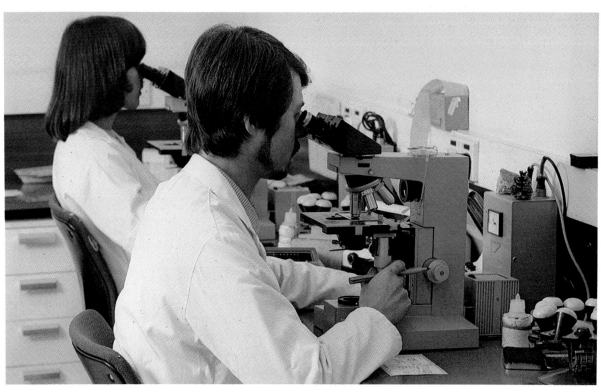

Blood is made up of different kinds of cells. Each type of blood cell has a different job to do. The cells travel around the body in a watery yellowish liquid called **plasma**. Plasma also has food parts, waste, salts, and other substances floating in it. Blood cells are made mainly in the tissue called **bone marrow**. Bone marrow is found in the middle of the long bones in your body.

Blood Cells

The most common kind of blood cells are the **red blood cells**. There are five million or more in a single drop of blood. New red blood cells are constantly being made in the bone marrow. It is the red blood cells that give blood its color. The cells contain a red coloring called **hemoglobin**. Hemoglobin is important because it carries oxygen and carbon dioxide. Red blood cells are like tiny rafts. They load up with oxygen in the lungs. On their journey around the body, they unload the oxygen. Then, they take carbon dioxide on board and flow back to the lungs again.

Another type of blood cell is the **white blood cell**. There are not nearly as many white blood cells as there are red ones. There are just one or two white cells for every thousand red blood cells. White blood cells are larger than red blood cells, and they can change their shape. Their job is to protect us from disease.

In the air around us, there are millions of very tiny creatures which can make us sick. These **germs** carry minor illnesses such as the common cold, as well as much more serious diseases. If we become sick, we usually get better before long. This is because white blood cells act as an army in our bodies which attack and destroy germs. White blood cells can grow in number very quickly. Some can change shape to surround the germs and "eat" them.

Sticking Together

If you cut your finger, you will begin to bleed. If the wound is a serious one, blood may pour out. Before long, however, the blood flow will slow down and stop. This is because of **platelets**. Platelets in the blood are smaller than other blood cells. They are also less numerous than red blood cells. In a sample of blood that has 1,000 blood cells, you would find about 200 platelets.

When you cut yourself and bleed, the body will try to fix itself. The platelets become sticky and they cling together. They slow down the blood flow. Then, they form a crust to protect the wound. This is called a scab.

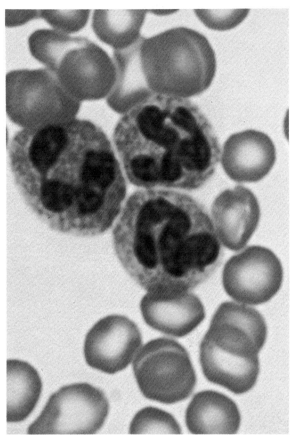

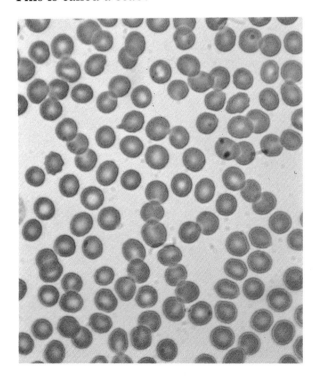

▲ The large cells in this picture are white blood cells. They are much bigger than the red cells around them. White cells defend the body against germs.

◀ Red blood cells are like round cushions which are thicker at the edges than they are in the middle. Capillaries are so small that the red cells have to squeeze through in single file. This is when they release their oxygen.

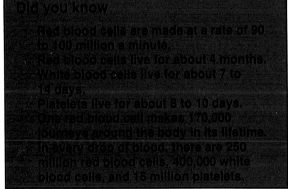

Did you know
- Red blood cells are made at a rate of 90 to 100 million a minute.
- Red blood cells live for about 4 months.
- White blood cells live for about 7 to 14 days.
- Platelets live for about 8 to 10 days.
- One red blood cell makes 170,000 journeys around the body in its lifetime.
- In every drop of blood, there are 250 million red blood cells, 400,000 white blood cells, and 15 million platelets.

Fighting Disease

There are two main kinds of germs. **Bacteria** are one kind of germ. They are very tiny and are found in many places. Many bacteria are useful to the body. They help the body break down waste material. But some bacteria do cause diseases. **Viruses** are even smaller than bacteria. Viruses make you sick when they get inside your body cells.

When harmful bacteria or viruses get into our bodies, white blood cells rush to attack them. If the white cells cannot destroy the germs right away, they make their own kind of poison for that particular germ. This poison is called an **antibody**.

Safe from Attack

When certain germs get into your body, your white blood cells start to make antibodies against them. It takes them a little time, so you might feel sick for a few days. But soon the antibodies kill the germs and you feel better. Also, once the antibodies are in your blood, they stay there forever.

Doctors can trick the white cells into making antibodies against certain diseases. They inject a dose of very weak or dead germs into the patient. This is called a **vaccination**. The dose of the virus is not enough to make the patient sick. However, it is enough to trick the white blood cells into producing antibodies against that virus. Those antibodies will then stay in the body. They will be ready if a strong version of the virus ever attacks the patient. The antibodies will kill that virus and the patient will not get sick.

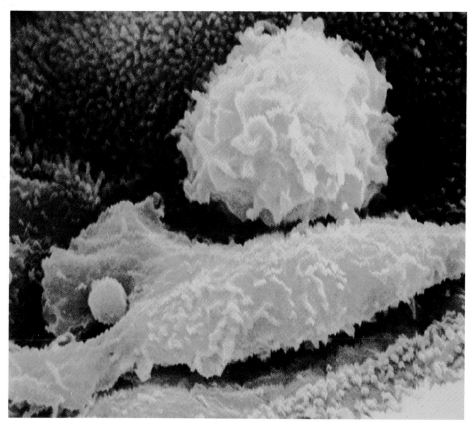

◀ The small round object is an attacking germ. A white blood cell is surrounding and swallowing it up. The cell destroys the germ, leaving only some waste matter. Waste such as this drains into the lymphatic system.

▶ Most children have vaccinations often, from the time they are babies onwards. The injection is over quickly and does not hurt much. Catching the disease would be much worse!

Cleaning the Blood

A clear, watery liquid called **lymph** also flows through our bodies. To do this, it uses a network known as the **lymphatic system**. All along the system there are bean-sized **lymph nodes**. A group of these nodes is called a **gland**.

There are extra white blood cells in the lymph nodes. The body uses the extra white blood cells from the lymphatic system to help it attack germs that have entered the body. When you are sick, you may have painful, swollen glands in your neck, armpits, and at the top of your legs. The swelling is the result of the battle between the germs and the white blood cells.

The Lymphatic System

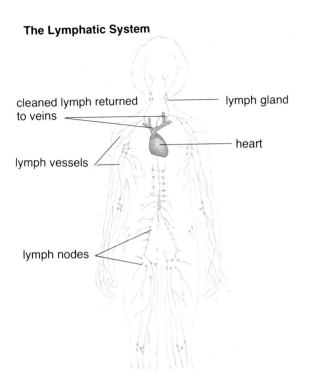

cleaned lymph returned to veins

lymph gland

heart

lymph vessels

lymph nodes

◀ Waste and extra fluid from the bloodstream are collected in the system of lymph vessels. These go all over the body. They clean the lymph and return it to the bloodstream near the heart.

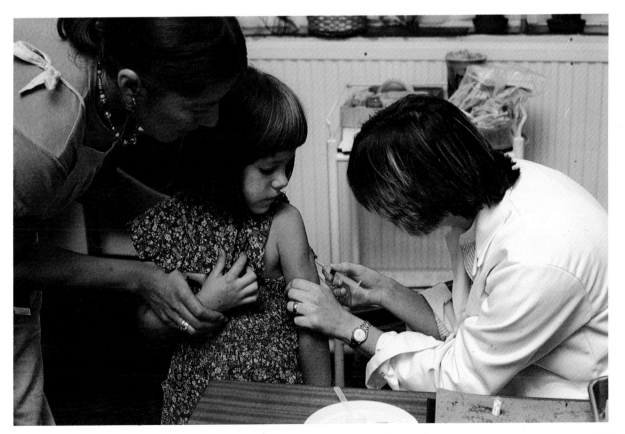

Fuel and Waste

A car needs gasoline to make it go. Our bodies need food for the same reason. The transportation system that takes food around the body is the blood.

Breakfast cereal, milk, bread, and everything else you eat has to be broken down into very tiny bits. The bits have to be small enough to get into your blood. This process is called **digestion**. It starts as soon as you start to chew your food. In your body there are substances which work with other things to make changes. These substances are called **chemicals**.

In your stomach, chemicals called digestive juices mix in with the food. They work on the food, breaking it down still further. The food then passes into a long tube called the **small intestine**.

The Digestive System

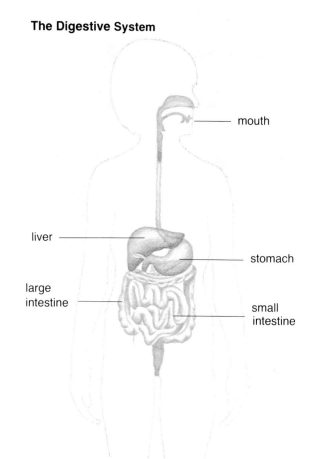

- mouth
- liver
- stomach
- large intestine
- small intestine

▲ The food we eat is broken into tiny bits by our digestive system. The useful parts are passed into the bloodstream. This carries the nutrients to every cell in our bodies.

▼ The inside of the small intestine is covered with villi. Nutrients pass through the villi into the blood. Then, this blood flows to the liver.

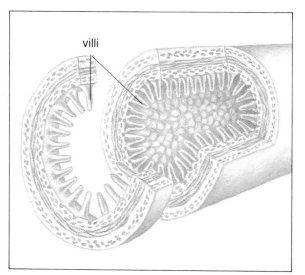

villi

The small intenstine is about twenty-three feet long. The inside walls of the small intestine are covered with tiny fingerlike **villi**. They give the intestine a very large surface area. If you streched the small intestine out flat it would cover a whole tennis court.

The villi contain many millions of blood capillaries. The walls of the villi are very thin. The nutrients from the food seep through the walls of the villi into the blood. Then, the blood travels all over your body to carry nutrients to the cells.

The Blood Filter

Down near the lower back are two important organs, your **kidneys**. Every day, the blood flows through the kidneys hundreds of times. The water in the blood is squeezed out and filtered. Unwanted waste matter and poisons are removed. The main waste is **urea**. This is made when food is digested. Too much urea in the blood is poisonous. The kidneys also filter out leftover medicine and alcohol.

Most of the water is put back into the bloodstream. Any water that the body does not need drains away into the **bladder**. The wastes and poisons are dissolved in the waste water. When the bladder fills up, we feel the need to go to the bathroom. This gets rid of the wastes filtered from the blood.

If the kidneys do not work properly, doctors need to use a kidney machine to take waste matter from the blood. One kidney is only as big as a fist. A kidney machine is as big as a closet, but it does not work as well as a real kidney.

More than half of our blood is made of water. The kidneys contain many tiny filters. The water passes through the filters and is cleaned. Most of the water goes back into the bloodstream again.

The Food Processor

The largest organ in the body is the **liver**. It has many different jobs to do. Blood flows from the intestines loaded with food. The first place it goes to is the liver. The liver stores much of this food. It can be sent out later to wherever it is needed.

Used red blood cells also end up in the liver. Any useful parts of them are stored, so they can be reused later.

How Water Is Passed from the Body

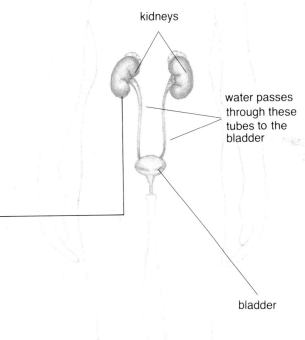

kidneys

water passes through these tubes to the bladder

bladder

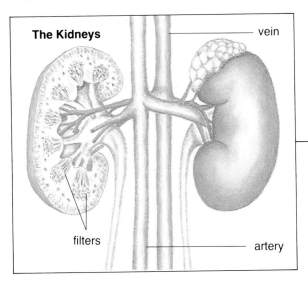

The Kidneys

vein

filters

artery

A Warm Body

Some animals rely on the sun to keep them warm. When it gets cold, their bodies slow down. They are **cold-blooded** animals. Humans and other mammals are **warm-blooded**. We make our own heat, so that our bodies always stay within a degree or two of the same temperature. This is important because it means we can stay active whether it is very cold or hot out.

Central Heating

When fuel burns on a fire or in a car, it makes heat. The same is true of the fuel our bodies take in. Most of the food we eat is used to make heat. Blood acts like the water in the pipes in a central heating system. Blood carries the heat, and spreads it all over the body.

At the center of the system is the liver which acts as the central heating boiler. The liver is helped by muscles. That is why we feel hot after running a race. The active muscles need extra food from the liver and when they use that food, it makes extra heat.

The muscles may sometimes be so active that we feel too hot. Blood then helps to cool us down. Tiny blood vessels near the skin get larger or **dilate**. We start to look red in the face. More blood comes to the surface of our bodies, and heat is given off into the air.

If we get too cold, blood vessels near the skin shut down. This keeps heat from

◀ This lizard is cold-blooded. This means that its body cannot make its own heat. When lizards are cold, they can only move slowly. They lie in the sun and soak up the heat like sunbathers. Humans are warm-blooded. Our bodies can make heat to keep us warm.

escaping through the skin. It makes the skin look pale or slightly blue. Shivering also helps. Tiny jerks by the muscles under the skin make the muscles work harder. This helps make extra heat to warm us up.

▶ Strip thermometers are useful for taking the temperatures of young children. They are placed on the forehead and kept there for one minute. N is for "normal." Mercury thermometers are usually placed under the tongue for a minute or two.

▼ After a hard workout, people feel hot. Sometimes, they sweat and their faces become red. This is because their muscles have been working hard. They have given off a lot of extra heat. Blood vessels fill up near the skin's surface. They give off heat through the skin and help to cool down the body.

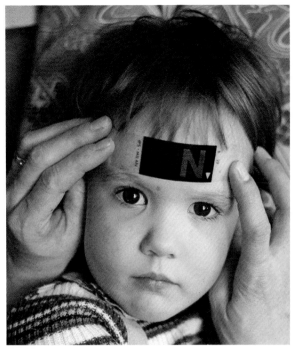

Taking Temperatures

The normal temperature of the body is about 98.6°F. This often rises when you are sick. Viruses seem to like the body's normal temperature. When the temperature rises, it is more difficult for the viruses to grow. Therefore, a higher temperature can mean that the body is fighting off an attack by germs. Unfortunately, a high temperature makes you feel tired and uncomfortable. Medicines can be used to help bring the body temperature down, so that you feel better.

Temperature is measured by using a **thermometer**. Body temperature is higher inside our bodies than on the surface of the skin. A mercury thermometer has mercury in it that expands as it warms up. The mercury moves along a narrow tube. The tube is marked off in degrees, which show different temperature levels. There is another kind of thermometer called a strip thermometer. This has tiny pieces of a special material in it which change color as they get warmer.

Body Control

Our bodies have their own patterns of activity and rest. Meals, work, playtime, and sleep all follow in the same order day by day. Chemicals called **hormones** play a large part in making the different parts of our bodies do the right things at the right times. Hormones are made in the **endocrine glands**. These glands are found near blood vessels. The glands pour their hormones straight into the bloodstream.

The Chemical Messengers

Hormones control how fast we grow, and when and how quickly we digest food. They also control how much water we keep in our bodies and our heart rate. Hormones tell certain cells to start working and others to stop or to go more slowly. Hormones may wash over every cell in the body, but each hormone has its own special target. It will cause changes in certain cells, but other cells will not be affected by it.

Body Changes

You can probably remember the feeling you get just before taking a test, or before the start of a race you really want to win. You might have a feeling like butterflies in your stomach. Your heart starts to thump in your chest. You breathe more deeply. All these things happen because of a hormone called **adrenalin**.

▶ The blood carries hormones which control the way in which our bodies develop. Some hormones are passed into the bloodstream by endocrine glands. Other glands bypass the bloodstream and make the hormone act directly on a part of the body.

the pituitary gland controls growth and some other glands

the thyroid gland controls the way our food is turned into energy

the thymus controls the way our bodies recognize germs

the adrenal glands control the way we react to fear

the pancreas controls glucose in the blood

the ovaries (in girls) and the testes (in boys) control the differences between females and males

Adrenalin acts on many parts of the body. It gets the body ready to run very fast or try very hard to do something. Before you even start to run a race, your heart is beating faster. It pumps extra nutrients and oxygen to your leg muscles, so that they are ready to work hard the moment you need them.

The hormone that controls the rate at which we grow is made in the **pituitary** gland, which is just below the front of the brain. It is very important that we have enough of this growth hormone.

▼ A race car driver waits for the start of a race. He feels tense and excited. The hormone adrenalin is working in his body. Adrenalin gives our bodies an extra surge of power when we are scared.

▲ We continue growing for about the first twenty years of our lives. The hormone that controls growth is made in the pituitary gland. People without enough growth hormone do not grow as fast as they should. They will be shorter than normal. Too much growth hormone means that they will grow taller than normal.

The Right Balance

Many different hormones flow around the body. There has to be just the right amount of each hormone to keep the body working properly.

For example, one hormone is called **thyroxin**. It is made in the **thyroid gland** which is in the neck. Thyroxin controls how fast we burn up food. People with too much thyroxin use up their food too quickly. They will be very thin and their heart rate will be faster than normal. If people's bodies do not make enough thyroxin, they will be fat and slow-moving. Too much or too little thyroxin makes people sick.

Healing

A cut or graze breaks the skin and the blood vessels under the skin. This causes the blood to leave the body. Blood is precious, so the body quickly takes action to stop the bleeding.

First, the platelets start to stick together. The blood gets thick and jelly-like. It forms a plug or **clot** which seals the hole.

This alone may be enough to stop the bleeding. At the same time, the blood vessels get narrower. This cuts down the amount of blood flowing to the cut, so that less blood will leak away.

Next, a scab forms. Chemicals in the blood near the clot make thin strands of a substance called **fibrin**. The fibrin grows into a cobweb-like net which traps more platelets and blood cells in it. Gradually, a solid scab builds up. It prevents dirt and germs from getting into the body. Meanwhile, the cells under the scab start to repair the damage.

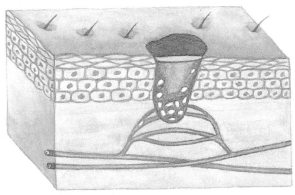

▲ Dirt and germs can get into a cut very easily. Blood flowing from the cut washes some of the germs away. White cells come to the wound and swallow up the remaining germs.

▲ When you cut yourself, platelets in your blood stick together. Strands of fibrin trap the platelets, and form a seal over the cut. This scab stops the bleeding.

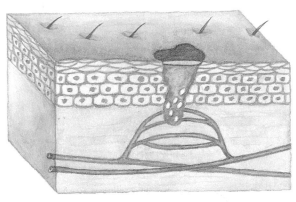

▲ New skin tissue starts to grow in order to repair the damage done by the wound. If the cut has been very bad, the new tissue may not grow back in the same way. It may leave a scar.

▲ When the skin is nearly healed, the scab falls away. Scabs should not be picked before they are ready to fall away. New cells may be damaged and germs may be let in.

Cleaning Up

The surface of your skin looks clean. In fact, it is covered with millions of bacteria. A cut lets in dirt and germs. The body must get rid of them as quickly as possible. White cells rush to the damaged area to swallow up the dirt and germs. Sometimes you see a yellowish liquid around a bad cut. This is **pus** which is made up of dead white cells and the waste they have swallowed up.

In just a few hours, a hard scab forms. Over the next few days, new skin grows under it. Once the skin has healed, the scab shrinks and drops off.

Bumps and Bruises

If the body is bumped or struck, it is often swollen and sore where it was hit. Later, a bruise appears. The bruise means that blood vessels under the skin have been damaged. Blood cells leak into the tissue under the skin. In a few days, white cells eat up these blood cells. The bruise is often blue, purple, or black. It fades to yellow before it disappears.

The area around a cut or bruise is often swollen. The swelling is painful, but it is part of the body's repair program. Blood vessels near the cut or bruise expand and leak. More blood can flow into the area to help it heal. Plasma and white blood cells seep into the nearby tissue.

▼ If you looked at a wound through a microscope, you could see the network of fibrin trapping the blood cells. This makes the blood clot. In this picture, the red blood cells have been shown in yellow so that they can be seen more easily.

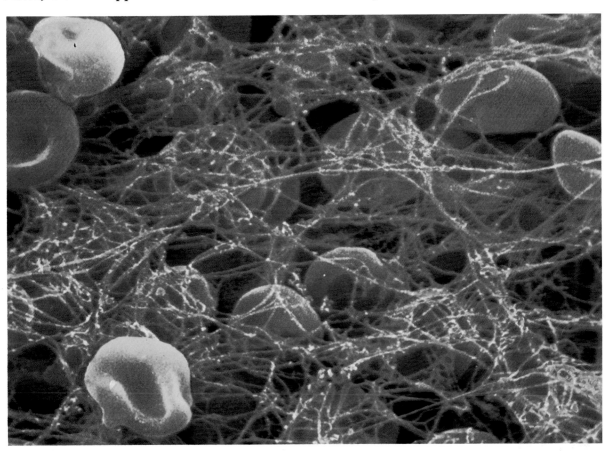

Blood Types

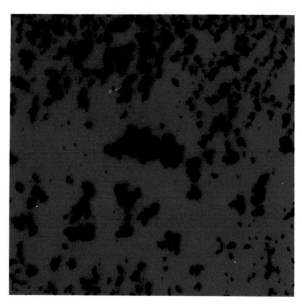

All blood looks the same under a microscope, but not all blood is alike. There are some substances that help the body to make antibodies. These substances are called **antigens**. Antigens are carried in red blood cells. However, the antigens in the blood of one person are not always of the same type as those in someone else.

Four Types of Blood

In 1900, an Austrian-American scientist named Karl Landsteiner figured out that there are four main groups, or types, of blood. He found out how the antigens of one blood type react with all the other types. He called the types A, B, AB, and O.

Blood in type A contains A antigens. It will make antibodies against B antigens. Type B contains B antigens. It will make antibodies against A antigens. Therefore, if A blood is given to someone with B blood, the B blood makes antibodies against the A blood. The antibodies from type B blood

will try to kill the cells in type A blood. A person can get very sick if this happens and might even die. Type O blood can be given safely to people with A, B or AB blood. However, type O people can only be given type O blood. Blood types that can mix safely are said to be **compatible**.

In 1940, scientists carried out tests with Rhesus monkeys and found a number of other substances. One of these, called the **Rhesus factor**, or Rh-factor, was found in the red blood cells of 85% of all people. These people have Rhesus positive blood. The other 15% are Rhesus negative.

If you are Rhesus positive and your blood is given to someone who is Rhesus negative, that person's blood would make antibodies to your blood. Those antibodies would stay in the other person's blood. If, later on, more Rhesus positive blood were given, the antibodies would destroy the red blood cells in the new blood. The new blood would then be useless.

Testing and Matching

Blood has to be carefully matched to make sure it will mix safely. The most common groups of blood are A, B and O types which are Rh positive. There are many more sub-groups as well, although they are much more rare. Scientists make careful tests and keep computer records. They are able to match people with rare blood groups who live thousands of miles apart.

► People from the same part of the world often have the same blood type. South American Indians, such as this family from Peru, often have blood type O. The Inca people, who once lived in Peru, learned to give blood transfusions hundreds of years ago. The operation was often successful because most Incas belonged to the same blood group.

▼ The victim of an accident is rushed to a hospital in an ambulance. If a patient is losing blood, doctors must quickly find out which blood type that person has.

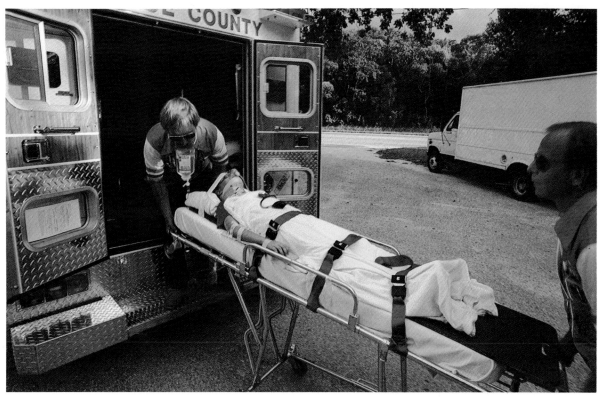

New Blood
for Old

A person who has had a bad accident might lose a lot of blood. If an artery is cut, the blood rushes out under pressure from the heart. The lost blood has to be replaced quickly. Blood from a healthy person is put into the veins of the accident victim. Doctors do this by giving a blood transfusion. People who have serious operations or something wrong with their own blood may also need transfusions of healthy blood. It is only during the last forty years that doctors have been able to do blood transfusions safely. They are now widely done and save millions of lives.

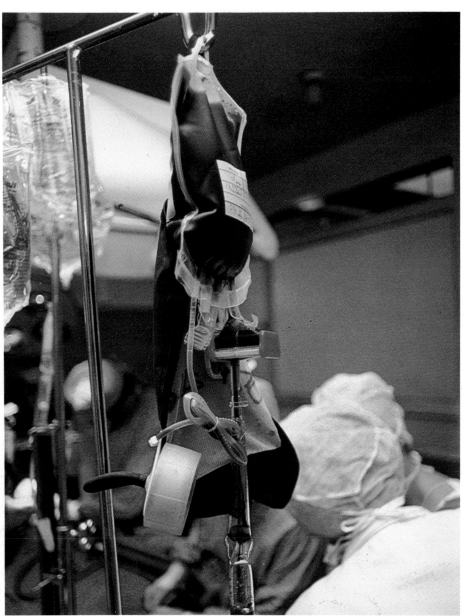

◄ A supply of new blood is given to a patient who is losing blood during an operation. The new blood will have been carefully checked to make sure that it is of the right type and that it is free from germs. Sometimes, many pints of blood are used during an operation.

34

Giving Blood

Healthy adults can give small amounts of their own blood without any harm to themselves. Someone who gives blood is called a **donor**. A donor can give about a pint of blood at a time without any problems. The body makes up the lost plasma in less than one day. It takes two to six weeks for the body to replace the lost red cells.

When a donor gives blood, a needle is put into a vein in the arm. It hurts no more than a pinprick. The blood flows along a thin tube into a container. The container has chemicals in it which keep the blood from clotting. It also has special food in it to keep the living cells alive.

The blood is then tested to find its type and to make sure it is not carrying any disease. After that, it is labeled and stored in a **blood bank** at about 40°F. At this temperature, it lasts for up to a month. After this, only the plasma can be used.

Often, blood is separated out into its parts, that is, plasma, cells, and platelets. This is because a patient may only need part of the blood. It would be wasteful to give the whole blood. For example, a patient may not have enough of his own platelets. The doctor will give him a transfusion containing just the plasma and platelets. The red and white cells can be used for another patient.

▲ Blood that has been taken from donors is stored in a blood bank. It must be ready for use at any time. Each container is labeled with details about the blood.

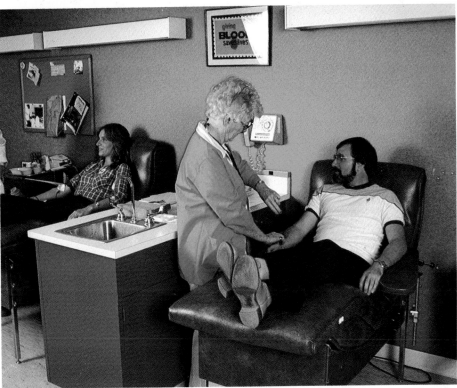

▶ Hospitals are always in need of supplies of healthy blood from donors. Giving blood can help save lives, and it does not harm the donor in any way.

Heart and Blood Diseases

Most hearts work very well for years and years. However, things can go wrong with the heart and circulation of the blood.

Sometimes, when a baby is born, the heart is not formed correctly, and cannot pump properly. Surgeons have to operate to take care of the problem.

As we get older, we may have trouble because of the way we live. For example, eating too much fat leads to fatty lumps in the arteries. The heart must pump harder to push blood through the half-blocked blood vessels. This causes strain on the heart and leads to sickness.

The heart itself needs blood that is rich in oxygen. The arteries that supply it are called the **coronary arteries**. If they get blocked, not enough blood gets to the heart. A **heart attack** follows. It is very painful, and the heart may stop beating. With quick treatment, the heart can often be restarted. Many people who have had heart attacks get better, but they must take care of themselves. Sometimes they need an operation to repair the coronary arteries.

▼ If we eat too much fatty food, our arteries become blocked. You can see what has happened in this picture. The blockage strains the heart and weakens it.

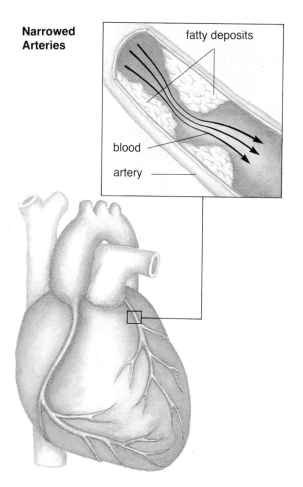

Narrowed Arteries

fatty deposits

blood

artery

▲ Modern medical treatment has made it possible for people suffering from hemophilia to lead active lives, although they must always be careful not to wound themselves. These youngsters are on a rock-climbing expedition in Wales.

Problems with Blood

Sometimes things go wrong with the blood. If people feel tired all the time and have no energy, they may have something wrong with their red blood cells. There may not be enough oxygen getting into the body cells. This is called **anemia**. It is caused when the body does not get enough **iron**. Iron is needed to make healthy red cells. Extra iron in tablets or in the right kind of food usually cures anemia.

Some boys are born with blood that does not clot properly. This problem is called **hemophilia**. For people with hemophilia, even a tiny cut could be dangerous because it is so difficult to stop the bleeding. Before blood transfusions were widely used, these people could not lead normal, active lives. Now they can get transfusions of plasma and platelets. This means that their blood will be able to clot if they cut themselves.

37

Making People Better

▼ Doctors can use an EKG to find out if the patient's heart is beating as it should. Electrical signals from the heart show up on the screen. Having an EKG test does not hurt.

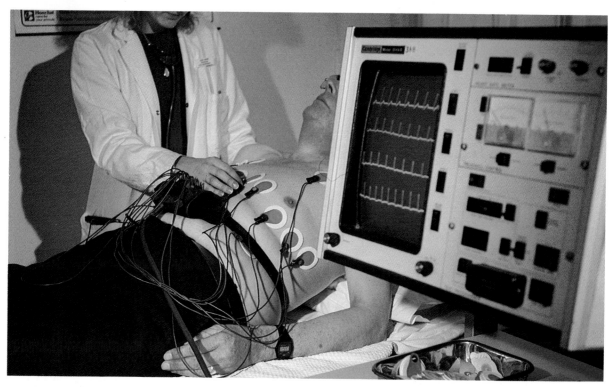

When people feel sick, they can go to doctors for advice. A doctor can tell a lot about the disease by asking questions. Patients can say if they have a pain, or feel tired, or out of breath. A stethoscope and blood pressure gauge help the doctor to make further checks. If the doctor thinks that the heart may be faulty, the patient can be sent to the hospital.

There are many machines in hospitals to help the doctor decide what is wrong. The patient's heartbeat can be recorded on an **electrocardiograph**, or EKG. A normal heart beats at a regular rate. Each time it beats, it sends out an electrical signal. Special pads are put on the patient's body. They pick up the electrical signals from the heart. The EKG machine turns the signal

into a wavy line, which it draws out on a computer screen. When the doctors study the line, they can see how its pattern differs from the pattern made by a normal heart. It helps them decide which part of the heart is not working correctly.

Open-Heart Surgery

Today, heart surgeons can correct all kinds of damage to the heart. Some babies are born with a hole in their hearts. This is a break in the wall that separates the heart chambers. The "hole" lets used blood mix with blood that has fresh oxygen. Also, the pressure in the heart is wrong, so it cannot pump properly. Forty years ago, many of these children died. Today, surgeons can operate to seal up the hole.

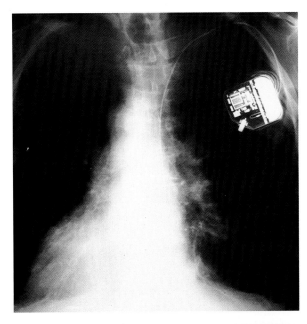

▲ This X-ray picture shows the inside of a patient's chest. On the right, you can see an artificial pacemaker for the heart. It has been put in during an operation.

New Parts

As we get older, our arteries may become clogged with fat. The arteries going to the heart itself may even become blocked. Surgeons can now replace the clogged artery with a blood vessel from a place that is not clogged, such as the leg, and transfer it to the heart. Artificial parts, such as a valve or pacemaker, can also be put in the heart to make it work better.

It is even possible to take out a faulty heart and put in a healthy one. This is called a **heart transplant**. The problem with this kind of operation is that the body does not like tissue that is not its own. Doctors must use powerful drugs to keep the body from rejecting the new heart.

▶ Samples are prepared for the microscope in a laboratory. Doctors take a sample of patients' blood in order to find out if they are suffering from any disease.

First Aid

When there is an accident, you can sometimes help someone before a doctor or a paramedic arrives. First aid may keep injuries from getting worse. Sometimes, it can save lives. An accident can be very frightening, even if you have not been hurt yourself. To give good first aid, you must stay calm, and know exactly what to do.

There are many places to learn first aid. You can find the telephone number of a local chapter of the Red Cross or your fire department in the telephone book. They are good places to go for information about first aid courses. Your school may even offer first aid courses.

▲ Someone with a heart attack has pain in the chest and maybe in the arms. They may collapse. You must get help right away. If there is no one nearby who can help, you must telephone the police or fire department and explain what has happened.

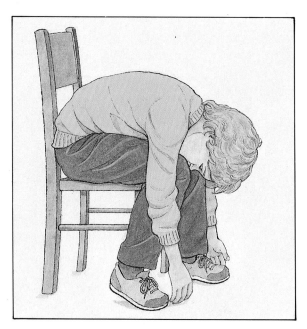

▲ When a person faints, they usually recover after a minute or two. Get the person to sit with his or her head between their knees. This gets the blood back to the brain and stops the feeling of faintness. If you are in a hot, stuffy place, open windows and doors, to let in fresh air.

▲ The blood vessels in your nose are delicate. A bump or even a change in the weather will often break a blood vessel, and make your nose bleed.
1 Pinch your nose gently to stop the bleeding. This gives the blood a chance to clot.
2 Do not tip your head back or the blood will go down the back of your throat.
3 Do not blow your nose for about half an hour after the bleeding stops.

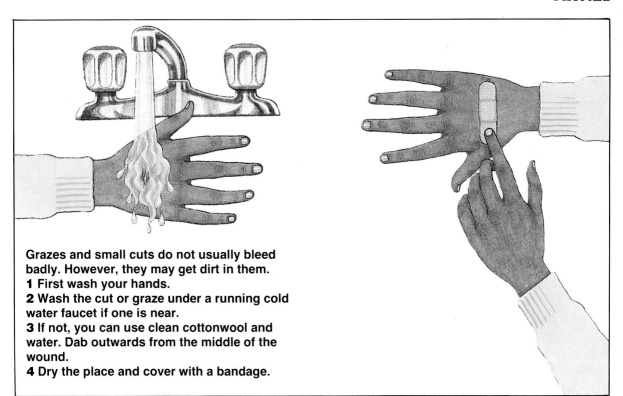

Grazes and small cuts do not usually bleed badly. However, they may get dirt in them.
1 First wash your hands.
2 Wash the cut or graze under a running cold water faucet if one is near.
3 If not, you can use clean cottonwool and water. Dab outwards from the middle of the wound.
4 Dry the place and cover with a bandage.

If blood keeps flowing out from a cut, it is serious. Get help from an adult right away. If there is no one else around, find a clean cloth. (Any piece of rolled-up cloth will do in an emergency.) Press it down hard on the wound. Keep pressing on the wound until someone comes.

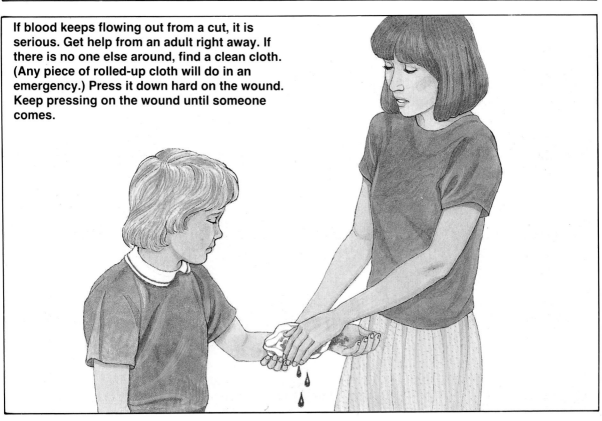

Health and Your Heart

Your body separates your food into nutrients. Different nutrients are used by the body in a different way. Too much or too little of a particular nutrient may be bad for you.

We know that many people get heart disease in the United States and many countries in Europe. It is much less common in the countries of Africa and Asia. The main reason for this is that the people of these countries eat a very different kind of diet than Americans and Europeans. In countries where there is more heart disease, the people eat much more fat and sugar, and less fruit and vegetables. This tends to make them fat, and to clog up their arteries. In the United States and Europe, even some very young children have been found to have the first signs of blocked or narrowed arteries.

The worst kinds of fats contain a substance called **cholesterol**. Most animal fats are high in cholesterol. Most vegetable fats contain very little. People should not eat too much fatty meat, butter, cheese, or eggs. They should eat vegetable-based margarine, low-fat cheese, and food cooked in vegetable oil.

The heart and blood need many nutrients to stay healthy. The blood needs iron to make red cells. It needs small amounts of **vitamins**. Iron is found in liver and green vegetables. Vitamins are found in many foods, but especially in fresh fruit and vegetables.

Smoking

Tobacco smoke contains many chemicals. These chemicals line the lungs with black tar. Often, smokers feel short of breath because their lungs are clogged and oxygen cannot get into the blood very easily.

Smokers get more chest infections and colds. The tar even makes their arteries become blocked more quickly. Smoking is very bad for your health.

◀ Our blood needs a supply of oxygen from the lungs. If we fill our lungs with cigarette smoke, instead, we damage our health. Smoking can kill you.

▼ People from Western countries must learn to eat better. They must eat balanced meals, with something from each food group. They especially need to avoid fatty foods that contain a lot of cholesterol.

▼ Donuts, cakes, and soft drinks do not make up a healthy diet. If we are to take care of our heart and blood, we should eat a variety of fresh foods, including fruit and vegetables. We should also drink fruit juice or water.

Staying Healthy

If your muscles are not used they get weaker and weaker. If you look at a dancer or an athlete, you will see that their muscles are firm and round. A person who never exercises at all has weak, flabby muscles.

The heart is a muscle like any other muscle in the body. The more it is used, the stronger it gets. Activities like running, skipping rope, and swimming will make your heart work. All these activities continue for a very long time, and they make your body need more oxygen. Your lungs work harder and your heart has to pump more strongly to send the blood to itself and to the other working muscles.

▲ A weightlifter may be very strong, but he may not be as healthy as a runner. Short bursts of exercise are not as good for the heart as longer-lasting exercise.

◀ Yoga is a kind of exercise which helps keep people limber and healthy. They also learn to breathe deeply. This brings oxygen into the bloodstream.

▲ Exercise is good for everyone. It keeps people in shape and healthy. Heart disease can start in young children. Exercise and the right kind of food will help you keep fit and healthy all your life.

When you exercise for the first time, you may feel tired. Next time you try it, it is not so bad. Your muscles, including the heart, get stronger. This is why athletes go into training. Each training session builds up the heart and lungs a little more. Gradually, the athlete becomes stronger.

The kind of exercise that works the heart and lungs is called **aerobic**. It means "with oxygen." Short, sharp bursts of exercise are not as good for the heart as continued aerobic exercise. Exercise like weight lifting or short sprinting are over before the heart really begins to work hard. That kind of exercise is called **anaerobic**, which means "without oxygen."

More people have cars than ever before. More people sit down and watch television than ever before. One reason why heart disease is increasing is that people do not get as much exercise as they used to.

A Healthy Life

Most people do not know that there is anything wrong with their heart and blood circulation until it is too late to do anything about it. Eating the right things and exercising regularly are not difficult. Lots of the food that is good for you tastes good, too. You do not have to go to a special class to exercise. Activities such as riding your bicycle, swimming, skipping rope, or playing tennis are all fun. It is nice to know that they are good for your heart, too.

Glossary

adrenalin: a substance in the body that helps the body to react quickly to danger. Adrenalin increases the amount of blood going to the heart, muscles, and brain.

aerobic: with oxygen. Aerobic exercise makes you use up oxygen more quickly than usual. It helps to build up the heart, lungs, and blood vessels.

alveoli: the tiny pockets covered with capillaries which make up your lungs.

anaerobic: without oxygen. Anaerobic exercise helps you to build up muscles, but does not exercise the heart, lungs, and blood vessels.

anemia: a blood disease. The blood does not carry enough hemoglobin or iron to supply the body. This makes people feel tired and weak.

antibody: a substance made by your body which protects it from disease. Each kind of antibody attacks a particular kind of disease.

antigen: a substance that gets into the blood from outside the body. Antigens cause the blood to produce antibodies to protect the body.

arteriole: a small tube through which the blood flows away from the heart to the body.

artery: a tube that carries fresh blood away from your heart and out to every part of your body.

atrium: one of the two small chambers at the top of your heart.

bacteria: tiny creatures that can only be seen with a strong microscope. Some are harmful and cause disease. Others are useful and help digest food.

bladder: the bag-like part of the body where waste liquid, or urine, collects.

blood: an important liquid found inside the body. It is red and carries food, oxygen and other important things to every part of the body.

blood bank: a place where blood that has been donated is stored.

bloodletting: making a sick person bleed to help them get well. Bloodletting was widely used before doctors understood how the body works.

blood pressure: the amount of force used by the heart to pump blood along the arteries and veins. It has two measurements: one when the heart is squeezing; the other when the heart is relaxed.

blood vessel: any tube which carries the blood through the body.

bone marrow: the substance inside bones where blood is made.

capillary: a very tiny tube which carries blood in and out of the body's cells. Capillaries are where arteries connect to veins.

carbon dioxide: a gas made up of carbon and oxygen. We get rid of it as waste when we breathe out.

cell: a very small part or unit. Most living things are made up of millions of cells.

chamber: an enclosed space. There are four chambers in the heart.

cholesterol: a fatty substance carried in the blood.

chemical: any substance which can change when mixed with another substance.

circulation: going around and around in the same space. Blood circulates around the body.

clot: when parts of a liquid cling together and the liquid stops flowing. When you cut yourself, the blood quickly clots and stops the bleeding.

cold-blooded: describes an animal whose body temperature is not controlled automatically.

compatible: to go with or fit with something else, such as when a substance mixes with another substance without any unwanted reaction.

coronary arteries: the blood vessels that supply blood to the heart, so that it can keep working.

diaphragm: a large muscle in the body that separates the chest from the stomach, and makes the lungs work.

digestion: the way food is broken down so that it can be used by the body.

dilate: to get large or wider. Blood vessels dilate to allow more blood to flow through them.

dissecting: carefully cutting up something to study how it is made and how the parts work together.

donor: someone who gives something to somebody else. A blood donor gives some of his or her blood to someone who needs it.

electrocardiograph (EKG): a machine which draws a graph of a person's heartbeat.

endocrine gland: a group of cells which make hormones to affect the behavior of other cells.

fibrin: a substance in the blood that helps the blood to thicken, so that it will not continue to flow out of a cut.

germ: a tiny living thing than can cause disease. Germs can only be seen with a strong microscope.

gland: a special group of cells which work together to make a substance for the body to use. Different glands make different substances.

heart: the part of the body that acts as a pump to push blood around the body.

heart attack: when the heart stops working, usually because the heart muscle is not getting enough oxygen.

heart transplant: when a diseased heart is taken out and replaced with a healthy heart.

hemoglobin: the substance which makes blood red. Hemoglobin carries oxygen.

hemophilia: a condition in which the blood is unable to clot.

hormone: a substance made in the body to cause changes, such as growth. Hormones are carried around the body in the blood.

humors: the four fluids, known as blood, choler, phlegm, and melancholy, which people used to believe were in the body.

iron: a mineral nutrient that our bodies need to stay healthy.

kidney: one of two parts of the body that clean the blood by taking liquid wastes from it.

liver: a part of the body with many functions. It stores useful food parts, keeps the body at the right temperature, and filters poisons from the blood.

lungs: the two sponge-like parts of the body used for breathing. Oxygen is taken into the body and waste gases are given off through the lungs.

lymph: a colorless liquid which carries white blood cells to the blood. Lymph helps in cleaning the blood and fighting disease.

lymphatic system: the tubes which carry a colorless liquid called lymph around the body to help clean the blood.

lymph node: places in the body where diseases and waste floating in the lymph are destroyed, and the fluid is cleaned before it goes into the blood.

microscope: an instrument that makes objects look many times larger.

muscle: tissue in the body which moves the bones to produce movement.

nutrient: the part of any food which can be used by the body for health and growth.

organ: a part of the body which has a particular job, such as the brain or stomach.

oxygen: a gas found in air and water. Oxygen is very important to all plants and animals. We cannot breathe without oxygen.

pacemaker: something in the body which sends out impulses to make the heart beat steadily. An electronic pacemaker can be placed in the heart if the natural pacemaker is not working properly.

pituitary gland: a part of the body which sends out substances to control growth and other changes. It is found beneath the brain, behind your forehead.

plasma: the clear, yellowish part of the blood. Plasma is mostly water. It carries the other parts of the blood in it.

platelet: a tiny particle in blood that helps make it thicken and clot.

pressure: the action of something pressing on, or against, something else.

pulse: a single beat of sound or light. The heart beats in a pulse.

pulse rate: the speed at which your heart is working to pump the blood around your body. Your pulse rate increases when you do exercise.

pus: a yellow liquid that is made when you get dirt and germs into a cut or wound. Pus is mostly dead white blood cells.

red blood cell: cells in the blood which carry oxygen and iron.

respiration: the way living things take in oxygen from air or water and get rid of carbon dioxide.

Rhesus factor: a substance found in some blood. Blood with the Rheseus factor (RH-factor) is called positive. Blood without the Rh-factor is negative blood.

ribs: a series of long bones which forms a cage around the heart, lungs, and other organs of the chest.

septum: a dividing wall in a plant or animal structure.

small intestine: the first part of the tube where food is absorbed into the body. It is a long, coiled tube that begins at the lower end of the stomach.

sternum: the long, flat bone in the center of your chest, to which most of the ribs are attached.

stethoscope: an instrument that a doctor uses to listen to sound in your body made by parts like the heart, the lungs, and the stomach.

thermometer: an instrument used to measure temperature.

thyroid gland: the part of the body which makes substances to control how the body uses energy. The thyroid gland is at the front of the neck.

thyroxin: the substance that controls how quickly food is used in the body.

tissue: many cells of the same kind acting together to do a particular job in the body. Muscles are made of muscle tissue.

transfusion: replacing unhealthy or lost blood with healthy blood.

urea: a waste filtered from the blood by the kidneys which is removed from the body in urine.

vaccination: giving someone a dose of specially treated germs that are not strong enough to give the person the sickness, but strong enough for the body to learn how to protect itself against them. The body can then protect itself against the disease in the future.

valve: a kind of tap or flap which opens or closes to let a liquid pass in and out of a pipe or tube.

vein: a tube that carries used blood full of waste gases from the body back to the heart and lungs.

ventricle: one of two pumping chambers in the lower part of the heart.

villi: tiny finger-like parts which line the inside of the small intestine.

virus: a kind of germ. They cause disease when they get inside the body's cells.

vitamin: a substance found in some foods. Tiny amounts of vitamins are needed by our bodies for good health and growth.

warm-blooded: describes an animal with a regular, stable body temperature.

white blood cell: a cell in the blood that fights disease.

Index